646.724

0746 033 842 4242

HAIR

Philippa Wingate

Designed and illustrated
by Kathy Ward

Hair consultant: Sally Norton
Photography by Howard Allman and Ray Moller
Series editor: Jane Chisholm
Series designer: Amanda Barlow

With thanks to Non Figg and Laura Fearn

CONTENTS

ABOUT THIS BOOK

The way your hair looks can make all the difference between going out with confidence or hiding at home. This book will help you make sure your hair always looks healthy and beautifully styled.

Find out how to put rollers in your hair on page 21.

There's advice on choosing a hair cut on page 6.

CHOOSING A STYLE

This book will help you to understand why your hair looks the way it does by describing its structure and how it grows. Find out how to choose a hairstyle that suits the shape of your face. There's also a guide to finding a reliable stylist and getting the most from your visit to a salon.

HAIRCARE

You will find out everything you need to know about looking after your hair, from shampooing and conditioning, to creating your own hair treatments from natural ingredients.

THE RIGHT EQUIPMENT

This book includes valuable information on how to choose the best tools to groom and style your hair, and a guide to using them safely and effectively.

PRACTICAL TIPS

There are tips on keeping your hair healthy and shiny with a balanced diet, and advice on protecting your hair all year round.

Techniques such as blow-drying and scrunch drying, plaiting and braiding, and curling your hair are described in straightforward, step-by-step stages.

Find out how to transform your hair for a special occasion by putting it up or adding temporary hair colourants and hair accessories.

HAIR INFORMATION

Charts on pages 28 and 29 will help you decide exactly what type of hair you have, and which hair products will suit you best.

On page 30 you'll find answers to some of the most frequently asked questions about hair, and there's a glossary on page 31 that will help you understand any hair words you might come across.

Find out how to create long-lasting curls in your hair on page 20.

UNDERSTANDING YOUR HAIR

To understand what your hair looks like, it helps to understand how it grows.

A HAIR'S STRUCTURE

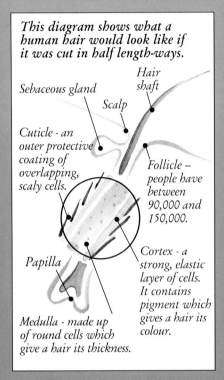

This diagram shows what a human hair would look like if it was cut in half length-ways.

Hair shaft

Sebaceous gland

Scalp

Cuticle - an outer protective coating of overlapping, scaly cells.

Follicle – people have between 90,000 and 150,000.

Papilla

Cortex - a strong, elastic layer of cells. It contains pigment which gives a hair its colour.

Medulla - made up of round cells which give a hair its thickness.

Each hair grows from a hole called a follicle. At the base of a follicle is a clump of cells called the papilla. The cells swell up and turn into hair cells. These then harden and die. As more are formed, the dead cells are squeezed out of the follicle to form the hair shaft.

Inside each follicle is a sebaceous gland. This produces an oily substance, called sebum, that coats your hair and keeps it healthy.

A hair grows about 12mm each month. It lives for between two and six years, after which it dies and falls out. Every day you will lose about 100 hairs, but new ones are constantly growing to replace them.

THICK OR THIN

The size of the follicles in your scalp determines the thickness of each hair. The larger the follicle, the thicker the hair.

Whether your hair is straight, wavy or very curly is determined by the shape of the shaft of your hair and the shape of your follicles. Straight hair has a round shaft and grows from a round follicle. Wavy hair has a round shaft, but it grows from a kidney-shaped follicle. A kidney-shaped follicle and an oval hair shaft produce very curly, black hair.

HEALTHY HAIR

If your hair is healthy, the cells that form the cuticle lie flat. This creates a smooth surface that reflects light well and makes your hair look shiny. When hair is damaged, the cuticles become cracked and frayed. They absorb light, making the hair look dull.

A healthy hair

An unhealthy hair

These strands of hair have been magnified hundreds of times.

A HEALTHY DIET

A well-balanced diet is essential for healthy hair. If your diet lacks certain nutrients your hair will soon begin to look dull and flat.

Make sure your diet includes the following:
- At least eight glasses of water a day.
- Low fat proteins. These are found in fish, seafood, cheese and eggs, nuts and seeds, and white meat such as chicken.
- Vitamins A, B and C. Vitamin A is found in milk, butter, eggs, fresh fruit and vegetables. Whole grain foods, such as oats and wheatgerm, contain vitamin B. Salads, raw vegetables and fresh fruit are high in vitamin C.
- Minerals. Good sources of zinc and iron are liver and vegetables. Milk and cheese contain lots of calcium.

REGULAR EXERCISE

To grow healthily, your hair needs a regular supply of oxygen and nutrients. These are carried to the hair follicles by your blood. To ensure a good supply of blood to your scalp, boost your circulation with exercise.

Seafood contains oils which will make your hair shiny.

Fresh fruit and vegetables are a valuable source of vitamin C.

Wholemeal pasta and bread help your body produce protein to strengthen your hair.

If you eat a healthy diet, you shouldn't need to take vitamin supplements like these.

Your diet should include three portions of vegetables every day.

Try to eat three pieces of fruit a day.

Milk, eggs and cheese, add essential protein to your diet.

Nuts are a good source of oil.

Pulses contain protein which strengthens your hair.

5

CHOOSING THE RIGHT HAIRSTYLE

The shape of your face is one of the most important things to consider when choosing a new hairstyle. A good cut will emphasise your good points and disguise the bad ones.

YOUR FACE SHAPE

To identify the shape of your face, use a headband to keep your hair off your face.

Stand in front of a well-lit mirror. With an old lipstick, draw around the outline of your face on the mirror. Carefully trace around the shape of your head, your cheeks and your jaw.

Compare the shape of your face with the shapes described in the chart below. The chart will then tell you which styles to choose and which to avoid.

Use an old lipstick to draw around your face on the surface of the mirror.

FACE SHAPE	CONSIDER	AVOID
OVAL Length equal to one and a half times the width at the cheeks	*This is considered the perfect face shape. Almost any hairstyle will flatter it. Straight, sleek styles, short cuts or dramatic swept-back styles will suit you.*	Don't let a stylist talk you into an outrageous haircut. It may suit the shape of your face, but it may not suit your lifestyle.
ROUND Almost as wide as it is long. Full near the cheeks	*Keep the sides of your hair sleek or short to make your face look narrower. Choose styles that brush forward and frame your face to make it look slimmer.*	Resist bubbly curls or full hair. Don't wear your hair swept back off your face. Avoid one-length cuts and hairstyles with a round outline.
LONG Narrow face with a long chin or a high forehead	*Your hair should be no longer than chin length. Curls at the sides of your face will add width. A fringe will make your face look shorter.*	Long, straight, one-length cuts, or hair pulled off your face, will draw attention to your chin and forehead. Don't choose a style without a fringe.
HEART Narrow at the jaw, wide at the forehead and cheeks	*Curls or waves at the level of your jaw will make it appear less narrow. A wispy fringe will make your forehead look narrower.*	A centre parting and a short fringe will make your forehead look broad. Fullness near your cheeks will make your chin look too narrow and pointed.
SQUARE Forehead, jaw and cheeks almost equal in width	*A side parting will make your face look less square. Choose a layered style that falls onto your face. A fringe will soften your hairline.*	Severe, angular haircuts, very short hair or hair pulled back off your face will draw attention to its shape. Avoid a centre parting.

CHOOSING A SALON

The best way to choose a salon is to ask friends whether they would recommend the salons they use. You can tell a lot about a salon from its appearance. Is it clean and tidy? Do you like the decoration? Don't choose anywhere that makes you feel uncomfortable or intimidated. Check that the charge for haircuts is within your price range.

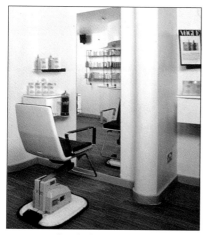

Visit a salon before you make an appointment. Check that it looks clean and hygienic.

A CONSULTATION

A good salon will offer you a free consultation. This is a chance to talk to a stylist and to take a closer look at a salon before you have your hair cut. Talk about how much time you spend styling your hair every day.

Try to have an idea of the style you want. Take along a photograph of a cut you particularly like. Most salons will have style books from which you can get ideas. Some salons may have a computer program called an imaging program which will will combine different hairstyles with a photograph of your face, so you can see whether or not a style will suit you.

An imaging program has created four dramatically different hairstyles for this woman.

LOOKING GOOD

Once you have had your hair cut in a style you like, go back every six to eight weeks for a trim to keep your hair looking its best.

A selection of the tools a stylist may use when cutting your hair.

Sectioning clips are used to clip sections of your hair out of the way.

A single-blade razor is particularly good for cutting short hair and for giving a softer shape to your hair than scissors can.

Electric clippers are used to cut hair close to the scalp.

Thinning scissors have toothed blades. They are used to reduce the thickness of your hair, without changing its length.

Cutting scissors have to be kept very sharp, because blunt blades will cut unevenly.

A stylist uses a comb to separate sections of hair.

SHAMPOOING YOUR HAIR

Shampooing your hair properly will noticeably improve its condition. If you follow the step-by-step guide on page 9, you will stamp out bad habits, such as using too much shampoo or not rinsing your hair adequately.

WHAT IS SHAMPOO?

Shampoo contains detergents which lift dirt and grease away from your hair so they can be rinsed off with water.

WHICH SHAMPOO?

There are shampoos that have been specially formulated for all types of hair, from greasy hair to dry hair, fine hair or curly hair. The charts on pages 28 and 29 will help decide what type of hair you have and which shampoo you should use.

You should shampoo your hair as often as necessary to keep it looking good and feeling clean. If you are using the right shampoo, you can wash your hair every day if you like without damaging it. It is not the frequency of shampooing that can damage hair, it is using a shampoo that contains too much detergent. Harsh shampoos will strip your hair of its natural oils. This may cause the sebaceous glands in your scalp to produce too much sebum to compensate. Your hair will soon begin to look lifeless, dull and greasy.

MAKE A CHANGE

From time to time, vary the shampoo you use, because your hair can become resistant to the ingredients in a particular shampoo.

When shampooing your hair, concentrate on the hair nearest to your scalp. The ends of your hair don't get very greasy.

SHAMPOOING YOUR HAIR PROPERLY

It is important not to use too much shampoo on your hair. Using more shampoo than you need will not make your hair cleaner, and can make your hair look dull. For short hair you'll need a dollop of shampoo the size of a grape. For long hair use a dollop about the size of a walnut shell.

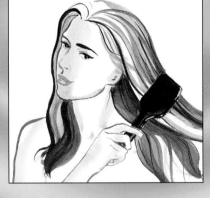

1. Before you start shampooing, brush your hair to loosen any dirt and dead skin cells. Then, lean over a basin or bath and wet your hair thoroughly with warm water.

2. Pour some shampoo into the palm of your hand and dilute it with water. Rub your palms together to work up a lather. Then, using your fingertips, massage the shampoo into your hair.

3. Massage your scalp with small circular motions to stimulate the blood circulation and encourage healthy hair. If your hair is longer than chin-length, don't pile it on top of your head and scrub at it. This will tangle it.

4. To rinse your hair, use a shower attachment or a cup with clean water from the tap. Never rinse with bath water as it contains flakes of skin and soap residue. Only shampoo again if your hair is very dirty.

5. Before you apply conditioner (see page 10), wrap a towel around your head or pat your hair with a towel to soak up any excess moisture. Don't rub your hair dry, as this can tangle it and cause damage.

CONDITIONING YOUR HAIR

Even healthy hair can be damaged by styling with heated appliances, brushing and combing, and extreme weather conditions, so always use a conditioner properly and regularly.

WHAT IS A CONDITIONER?

A conditioner contains substances that will add moisture to your hair and strengthen it. It will also make your hair look more shiny.

WHICH CONDITIONER?

Conditioners are available for all hair types in a variety of forms. The charts on pages 28 and 29 will help you choose one to suit your hair.

Light conditioning rinses make normal hair shiny and easy to comb.

Creamy, oil-based conditioners are good for dry hair.

Conditioning mousse can be left in your hair.

Use intensive conditioners to treat damaged hair.

Apply a conditioner to towel-dried hair. Wet hair will dilute a conditioner and make it work less effectively.

HOW DOES IT WORK?

Shampooing may make the cuticles of your hair ragged. They can interlock with the cuticles of other hairs, causing tangles and knots. A conditioner will coat each hair shaft and smooth down the cuticle, making your hair less likely to tangle. The flattened cuticle will reflect light better, so you hair looks shinier when it is dry.

Follow the manufacturer's instructions about how to apply a conditioner and leave it on your hair for the time recommended. Leaving a conditioner on longer won't necessarily make it work better.

APPLYING A CONDITIONER

1. Apply a conditioner to clean, towel-dried hair. Short hair needs a tablespoonful of conditioner; long hair needs about two. Massage the conditioner into your hair, concentrating on the ends, and distribute it with a comb.

2. Rinse your hair until the water running off it is completely clear. It is very important to rinse thoroughly, as a build up of shampoo and conditioner on your hair can leave it looking dull and lifeless.

3. Pat your hair dry with a towel. Wet hair is fragile and stretches easily, so it is important not to pull or tug it. Comb it through gently with a wide-toothed comb, starting at the ends and working up to the scalp.

HOLIDAY HAIRCARE

Holidays can be a very damaging time for your hair, so you need to take extra care to protect it.

SUMMER HAIRCARE

The sun dries the moisture and oils in your hair, leaving it brittle and lifeless. You can buy gels and sprays containing a sun-screen that will protect your hair. Alternatively, cover your hair with a hat or a scarf. After swimming, rinse your hair to get rid of sea salt or pool chemicals that can spoil your hair's condition.

WINTER HAIRCARE

Cold temperatures, central heating and the wind can leave your hair dry and tangled. Keep it tied back if it is long enough and always wear a hat outdoors. If wearing a hat makes your hair greasier than usual, wash it daily with a mild shampoo.

In damp weather, use gel or hairspray to coat your hair with a thin, protective layer. This will stop moisture in the air from penetrating your hair and making it frizzy.

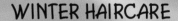

TREAT YOURSELF

For generations, people have used natural products, such as lemon juice and eggs, on their hair. Here are the recipes for some effective shampoos and conditioners you can mix up yourself. However, make sure you use the treatments immediately, otherwise the ingredients they contain will go bad.

Cider vinegar

Olive oil

Eggs

You'll find ingredients in the kitchen that you can use to improve the condition of your hair.

EGG SHAMPOO

Egg is an excellent cleanser. It clings to dirt and, when you rinse your hair, it drags the dirt away with it. The protein in egg acts as a conditioner.

To make egg shampoo, beat together the white and yolk of an egg in a mixing bowl. Massage the mixture into dry hair and leave it for about five minutes. Rinse your hair thoroughly in cool water.

MAYONNAISE CONDITIONER

Mayonnaise contains eggs, oil and vinegar which will make your hair beautifully shiny and conditioned. You can buy mayonnaise or make your own.

To make mayonnaise, mix a tablespoon of vinegar, and an egg yolk. Stir in eight tablespoons of olive oil. Beat the mixture until it becomes creamy. Smooth it over your hair, and leave it on for five minutes before shampooing it out.

WARM OIL TREATMENT

Treat damaged, dry hair with this warm oil treatment.

Put two tablespoons of olive oil in a cup. Place the cup in a bowl of hot water for a couple of minutes, until the oil has been gently heated. Massage the oil into your hair.

Wrap a piece of clingfilm around your hair, and scrunch it up to seal the ends together. Wrap a towel around your head, and leave the oil on for 30 minutes before shampooing it off. Finally, rinse thoroughly.

QUICK RINSES

Give your freshly washed hair extra body, brightness or shine by applying a rinse. Here are some simple ones you can make:

● **Lemon juice** is particularly good for brightening blonde hair. Add four teaspoons of lemon juice to a litre of cool water and pour it over your hair as a final rinse.

● **Vinegar** gives dark hair extra shine. Add half a cup of vinegar to a litre of water and pour it over your hair. Rinse your hair thoroughly, to make sure it doesn't smell.

INFUSIONS

Some herbs or plants can be used to cure various problems and improve the condition of your hair. Different herbs have different effects, but don't use anything unless you are sure what it is.

To make an effective herbal rinse, known as an infusion, place 25g of your selected herb in a container and pour over 300ml of boiling water. Close the container and leave the herbs to soak in a warm place for several hours. (The longer they soak, the stronger the effect will be.) Finally strain the liquid and pour it over clean, wet hair.

An infusion of sage leaves prevents static electricity from building up in your hair.

Marigold petals will brighten red tones in auburn hair.

An infusion made from nettles will soothe an irritated scalp.

Lavender removes excess oil from your hair and scalp.

Rosemary stimulates hair growth.

An infusion of camomile flowers lightens blond hair and adds shine to dull hair.

BLACK HAIR

Black (Afro-Caribbean) hair is often very dry and fragile. As a result, it needs gentle styling and special care to look its best.

STRAIGHTENING HAIR

A hair straightener or relaxer is a chemical solution. When it is applied to curly hair, it changes the structure of the hair, breaking the bonds that form curls so they can be reformed into a straight pattern.

The process stretches the hair shaft and can cause damage, so always have this done by a professional. Straightening is permanent, and only has to be repeated when new, curly hair grows.

EXTENSIONS

Hair extensions are made of real hair or strands of nylon fibre. They are attached to a person's natural hair using glue or heat to form a seal. They should only be attached by a professional hairdresser.

Extensions come in almost any texture or colour, and are great for adding length and volume to your hair.

BRAIDING

Braiding is a technique in which hair is divided into lots of tiny little plaits which can be arranged in various styles. Braids can be left in place for up to two months.

This girl's hair has been braided and then extensions of long spiral curls have been added.

Braids can be decorated with colourful beads.

Care should be taken when braiding. If your hair is pulled too tight the follicles can be damaged, which may make your hair break or fall out.

CARING FOR BLACK HAIR

Black hair is usually very curly. The curls allow moisture to escape the hair shaft, and they make it difficult for the natural oils to travel down the hair shaft. This makes the hair dry and fragile.

Here are some tips on looking after it:

● Use a gentle shampoo and a rich conditioner when washing your hair.

● Give your hair a moisturising warm oil treatment (see page 12) once a month.

● Regular combing will spread the natural oils through your hair, making it look shinier and healthier.

HAIR ACCESSORIES

Accessories are great for dressing up your hair. You can buy a wide selection from department stores or supermarkets.

Bendies are flexible lengths of wire covered in tubes of fabric. Twist them to secure them in position.

Covered bands will not damage your hair like rubber bands.

Hairpins can be used to secure chignons and buns.

Kirby grips

A zig-zag headband

Hair combs

Claw clips will grip your hair firmly.

Scrunchies are elastic bands covered in tubes of material. They are used to keep ponytails and plaits in place.

Silk flowers attached to a hair comb

Slides, also called barrettes, will clip your hair into place. They come in all shapes, colours and sizes.

Snap hair slides are easy to use.

Diamante slides add sparkle for nights out.

If you wear your hair up, you can dress it up with decorative pins.

BRUSHES AND COMBS

A brush and comb are the basic equipment you need for everyday styling and haircare, so it is important to choose the right tool for the job.

This rubber base can be removed for cleaning.

Styling brushes are probably the most useful brushes. They can be used for blow-drying and grooming.

Many brushes have rubber balls on the tips of the bristles so they do not scratch your scalp.

Grooming brushes have bristles set into a flexible rubber pad which ensures they don't pull your hair.

Radial or circular brushes are round styling brushes. They can be used to create curls or flick up the ends of your hair when you blow-dry it.

A smaller radial brush produces a tighter curl.

BRUSHES

Brushes can have a variety of types of bristles: natural hog bristles, nylon, plastic or metal bristles, or combinations of these types. The bristles are embedded in a handle made of wood, plastic or rubber.

When you buy a brush, choose one with long, widely spaced bristles that will not get tangled in your hair. The smoother and blunter the bristles, the kinder they will be to your hair. Avoid brushes with metal bristles that do not have rubber balls on the tips, as these can scratch your scalp.

To check that the bristles on a brush are not too sharp, press the brush into the palm of your hand. If it hurts your hand, look for a brush with blunter bristles.

Paddle brushes are square in shape and good for grooming long hair.

Vent brushes are good for blow-drying because they have holes, or vents, along the back. These let hot air pass through them. Vent brushes can be flat or round.

COMBS

Make sure you choose a good quality, plastic comb. Look for one with "saw-cut" teeth, which means each tooth is individually cut into the comb. These don't have sharp edges that tear your hair. Cheap plastic combs are made in moulds, and often have rough ridges on the teeth which can damage your hair.

KEEP IT CLEAN

To keep your brushes and combs clean and hygienic wash them every two weeks.
- Use a comb to remove any loose hairs clogging your brush.
- Use an old toothbrush to remove any grease and dirt that builds up on the base of the brush and its bristles.
- Wash brushes and combs in soapy water which contains a drop of antiseptic. Rinse them well, shake off any excess water, and let them dry naturally.
- Check your brushes and combs for signs of wear and tear. Buy new ones if you notice they have rough edges or damaged teeth and bristles.

Wide-toothed combs are ideal for wet hair, which is very fragile. They will not stretch or break your hair.

Use a wide-toothed comb to detangle curly or permed hair.

A mousse comb has two rows of teeth. It is used to distribute styling products evenly through hair.

The tail can be used to create a parting or to separate sections of hair for blow-drying or when using rollers.

A tail comb has fine teeth for grooming hair and a long, pointed tail made of metal or plastic.

This grooming comb has wide teeth for grooming and fine teeth for fine hair.

Afro combs have long, widely-spaced teeth. They are ideal for use on black or permed hair. Some afro combs have a combination of widely spaced teeth and fine teeth.

These fine teeth can be used to smooth any tufts of hair that grow at the hairline.

DRYING YOUR HAIR

You can improve the shape and volume of your hair by using the correct styling products and blow-drying technique.

HAIR DRYER

To dry your hair in a hurry, or style your hair while you dry it, a hair dryer is an essential piece of equipment.

A diffuser spreads out the airflow so hair can be dried more slowly. Ideal for curly hair.

Switch to adjust the temperature

Select a dryer that has adjustable temperature and speed settings like this one.

Switch to adjust the speed

Use clips to separate sections of your hair as you dry it.

A nozzle attachment fits over the end of a dryer to direct the airflow more precisely.

STYLING PRODUCTS

You can use a styling product on your hair before drying, to add volume. Some products will sculpt your hair when it is dry. Follow the instructions on the container. Never use too much of a substance as it can make your hair look dull. Here are some of the products available.

PRODUCT	DESCRIPTION	COMMENT
Setting lotion	*Liquid applied to towel-dried hair before using rollers.*	Helps your hair to hold the curl produced by rollers. Can leave hair a feeling a little hard.
Blow-drying lotion	*Liquid applied to towel-dried hair before blow-drying.*	Protects hair from the heat of a dryer. Similar to setting lotion, but leaves hair feeling softer.
Mousse	*Foam used on wet or dry hair.*	Adds body and texture. Good for scrunch drying (see opposite). Conditioning mousses are best.
Gel	*Transparent jelly or spray applied to dry or damp hair.*	Used to sculpt hair. Wet-look gel will mould your hair into dramatic positions. Messy to apply.
Hairspray or **fixing spray**	*Fine, quick drying varnish that holds styled hair in place.*	Comes in a variety of "holds" (how stiffly the hair is held). Dries hair if left in too long.
Waxes, creams and **pomades**	*These come in different forms, but all are applied to dry hair.*	Will make curly hair less frizzy and give straight hair a more tousled look.
Glosses, serums or **shine sprays**	*Fine liquids that coat the cuticle of your hair with oil or silicone.*	Make hair look healthy and shiny. Particularly good on black hair and for sleek, smooth styles.

A GUIDE TO PERFECT BLOW-DRYING

If you want to blow-dry straight or wavy hair into a smooth, sleek shape, follow the step-by-step guide below.

Don't start with dripping wet hair. Dry it with a towel or give it a blast of warm air with your dryer to remove excess moisture. Spread a little styling product through your hair to protect it from the heat of the dryer.

Clip the hair you are not working on out of the way.

Hold the dryer about 10cm from your hair.

Keep the dryer moving so it doesn't scorch your hair.

1. Blow-dry small sections of your hair at a time. Starting at the back of your head, dry the lower layers first. Work your way round to the sides and finish with the top of your hair and fringe.

2. To dry each section, place a brush at the roots of your hair, and pull it through to the ends. Point the airflow from the dryer down the hair shaft. This will make the cuticle lie flat, so your hair looks shiny.

3. Curve the ends of your hair around your brush to give them a little curl. A final blast of cold air will help your hair hold its shape.

SCRUNCH DRYING

Scrunch drying will maximize the curl in curly or wavy hair.

First, apply plenty of mousse to freshly washed, towel-dried hair. Tip your head forwards and blow the roots of your hair with a dryer. This will help to create volume. Then, keeping your head tipped forwards, squeeze handfuls of your hair in your fist as you dry it.

Don't brush your hair after drying – this will pull out the curls you have created.

This girl is scrunch drying her hair.

You can use a styling product, called a curl revitalizer, to increase the curl in your hair.

Attach a diffuser to your dryer. This will allow warm air to dry your hair without blowing out the curls.

CREATING CURLS

Whether you want to create tight curls or just add waves to make your hair look thicker, the basic tools and techniques you will need are the same.

HOT CURLS

The heat produced by heated appliances will curl your hair quickly and effectively. There are a wide range of different tools available. Some of the main tools are shown above.

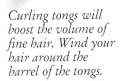

Curling tongs will boost the volume of fine hair. Wind your hair around the barrel of the tongs.

Use heated brushes to smooth hair or to curl it. Keep the brush wound into your hair for 5 seconds.

A crimper and straightener has two reversible metal plates. One side is ridged to give hair a crinkled effect. The other is flat and will smooth curly or frizzy hair.

Heated rollers come in sets which contain different sized rollers for different sized curls. The rollers are heated on metal posts.

CURL WITH CARE

- Before using heated appliances always read the manufacturer's instructions.
- Heated appliances dry and damage your hair, so don't use them as part of your daily styling routine. Always use a styling product to protect your hair from the heat.
- Avoid leaving them in your hair for longer than necessary, as you may scorch it.
- Never use plug-in appliances with wet hands or near water. They can give you a serious electric shock.
- Always unplug or switch off appliances after use.

For curls that keep their shape longer, create the curls with a heated appliance, then allow your hair to cool completely before you brush or comb it through.

USING ROLLERS

Rollers are a good way to add volume to your hair. Follow the steps below to put in heated or cold rollers. To use cold rollers your hair should be slightly damp, and to use heated rollers it should be completely dry.

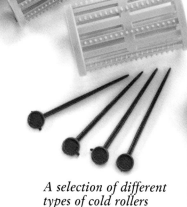

Wind-in rollers have to be secured with pins.

A selection of different types of cold rollers

Bendy foam rollers will produce soft, spiral curls. Wind your hair around a roller and lift the ends up to fix it in position.

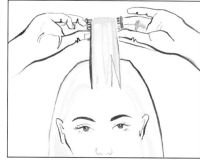

1. Starting at the front of your head, comb a section of hair upwards, away from your scalp. Small sections are easiest to work with.

2. Wrap the ends of your hair around the roller neatly. Wind the roller down towards your scalp, taking care not to get it tangled in your hair.

Velcro rollers come in a variety of sizes and shapes. They are easy to use. They grip your hair, so you don't need pins to fix them in place.

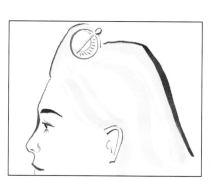

3. To secure a wind-in roller, push a pin through it. Heated rollers have pins or clips to fix them in position. A Velcro roller grips your hair by itself.

4. Repeat the process described in steps 1 to 3 until you have worked your way around your whole head.

Some Velcro rollers are ball-shaped.

TAKING ROLLERS OUT

You should leave heated rollers in your hair for about 20 minutes, until they are cool. Leave cold rollers in until your hair is dry. Finally, remove the rollers and comb your hair through.

A DASH OF COLOUR

Whether you want a hint of colour or rainbow stripes, these pages will tell you all about colouring your hair.

HAIR COLOURANTS

Colourants work by staining the hair shaft (see page 4) with colour. The length of time a colour lasts depends on how far the colourant penetrates into the hair shaft.

When you buy a colourant, there will be information on the packet about what type of colourant it is

Using two or more temporary colours in your hair can produce a dramatic effect.

and how long the colour will last. Follow the manufacturer's instructions carefully. Leave a colourant on for the exact time specified. This will ensure the colour develops properly.

There are three main types: temporary, semi-permanent and permanent.

Temporary colourants coat the surface of your hair shaft with a thin layer of colour. This will be washed away after one or two shampoos. So, if you want to experiment with colouring your hair at home, temporary colourants are the safest to use.

Semi-permanent colourants actually penetrate the outer cuticle of your hair and coat the cortex. They can last for between six and eight shampoos. The colour will fade gradually.

There is also a longer lasting type of semi-permanent colourant.

Temporary and semi-permanent colourants come in many different forms. Here is a selection.

You can add streaks of colour with hair lipsticks.

These penetrate deeper into the cortex of your hair and last for up to 24 washes.

You can use semi-permanent colours to add brighter, richer tones, or to darken your hair. They can only lighten the colour of your hair very slightly.

Permanent colourants contain a chemical, such as hydrogen peroxide, which opens up the hair cuticle and allows a coloured dye to penetrate deep into the cortex. They come in liquids or creams with a separate container of hydrogen peroxide. The two components have to be mixed together before use.

The colour doesn't wash out, it grows out. If you want to keep the colour, you'll have to reapply it to the roots of your hair about every six weeks.

Permanent colourants chemically alter the structure of your hair, which can cause damage. So always have them applied by a professional.

Brush hair mascara through your hair with the wand provided.

Add sparkle to your hair with hair glitter.

BLEACHES

Bleaches don't add colour to your hair, they remove it. They contain a chemical, such as hydrogen peroxide, that lightens your hair by removing colour from the cortex. If left on long enough, bleach will turn your hair almost white. For a more natural look, people often add a golden or silver colour to hair that has been bleached.

CHOOSE A COLOUR

To ensure that a colour suits your complexion, select one close to your hair's natural shade. For example, if your have a pale complexion don't use a colourant that is too many shades darker.

Before using a permanent colourant, experiment with a temporary colourant first.

TESTING COLOURANTS

The colour a colourant produces and the length of time it lasts differs from one person's hair to another's. For example, a temporary colour used by someone with bleached hair will be harder to wash out, because bleached hair absorbs colour rapidly.

Always perform the following tests to check that your hair and skin reacts well to a colourant. If you have any doubts consult a hairdresser.

Strand test – To check that your hair reacts well to a colourant and that you like the colour, do a strand test. Pin the top layer of your hair out of the way and apply the colourant to a lock of hair from the lower layers which don't usually show.

Hair mascara looks dramatic and should wash out with just one shampoo.

Leave it on for the time recommended by the manufacturer before rinsing.

Skin test – Dab a little colourant on to the skin on the inside of your elbow. Leave it for a few hours. If your arm begins to itch or turns red, don't use the product.

You can buy semi-permanent colourants in vivid shades as well as natural tones.

Spray-on colours will wash out of your hair easily.

Some shampoos and conditioners contain colourants.

Semi-permanent colourant mousses are easy to use.

Semi-permanent colourants come in creams and liquids.

23

PARTY STYLES

Whether your hair is long or short, you can transform it for a special occasion. Here are three looks that are quick and easy to create.

Just follow the step-by-step instructions. You can decorate party hair with slides or temporary colourants.

A SPIKY CHIGNON

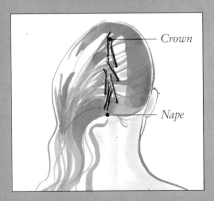

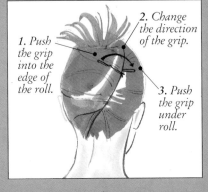

1. Brush one side of your hair back and to the side as shown above. At the centre of the back of your head insert a row of kirby grips, from the nape of your neck to your crown.

2. Gather your hair into a low ponytail. Lift up the ponytail and twist it towards the pins, until it forms a roll at the back of your head. Allow the end of your ponytail to flop forwards.

3. Use kirby grips to secure the roll. Push each grip into the edge of the roll. Then, changing the direction of the grip, catch a piece of the rest of your hair and push the grip under the roll.

MINI TWISTS

1. Divide your hair into neat sections. Twist each section until it begins to twist back on itself.

2. Secure each twist with two kirby grips crossed over each other. Allow the ends of each twist to remain spiky.

3. If your hair is too short at the sides to twist, use gel to smooth it flat. Use hairspray to hold your hair in position.

A spiky chignon combines a sophisticated twist with a wild, spiky top.

Spray the spiky top with hairspray to hold it in place.

SNAKE TWISTS

Add streaks of hair mascara (see page 22) to your mini twists for a really funky party look.

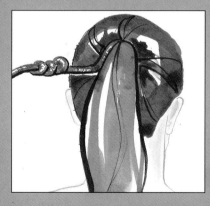

1. Brush your hair into a ponytail at the back of your head. Secure it with a covered band.

Two or three matching slides make stylish decorations.

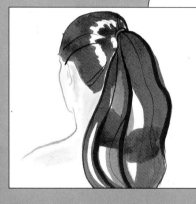

2. Pull small sections of hair free from the outer edge of your ponytail. Twist each section until it begins to twist back on itself.

Catch hair from the twist and the rest of your hair as you push the grip in.

3. Using a kirby grip, pin each twist to your hair, above the covered band. You can create as many twists as you like.

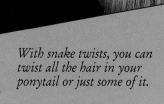

With snake twists, you can twist all the hair in your ponytail or just some of it.

PLAITING AND BRAIDING

Whether your hair is long, short, straight, wavy or curly, you'll be able to create one of the styles shown on these pages. They are not as hard as they look. A little practice will quickly make you into a fantastic braider.

Decorate your braids with scrunchies and covered bands, or add brightly coloured embroidery threads in contrasting colours.

A FRENCH PLAIT

Blend the new hair with the section.

1. Take a section of your hair from the front of your head and divide it into three parts.

2. Plait your hair once, by taking the right section over the middle one and the left over the middle section.

3. Gather up a thin strand of the loose hair next to the right section and one next to the left section. Join the new strands in neatly with each section and plait them once.

The more you practice a French plait, the neater it will look.

Covered bands and scrunchies come in all kinds of sizes and thicknesses. Use a small one for a fine plait and a larger one to secure a chunky plait.

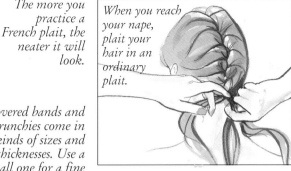

When you reach your nape, plait your hair in an ordinary plait.

4. Continue plaiting in this way, taking a strand of hair from each side to join in with the plait. At the end, secure the plait with a covered band.

HIPPIE BRAID

For a three-colour hippie braid, you need three pieces of embroidery thread that are about two and a half times longer than your hair. Tie them together with a knot at one end.

This braid has been bound with three colours of thread.

1. Separate a section of hair near the front of the head. Loop the knotted end of the thread around the section and tie the thread securely in a knot around the hair.

Tie a knot at the ends of your embroidery threads.

You could put several hippie braids in your hair at once.

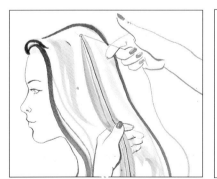

2. Lay two of the threads along the section of hair, and start to wind the third one neatly around both the hair and the threads.

3. After binding about 5cm, swap the threads over, so you are binding with one of the threads which was lying along the hair.

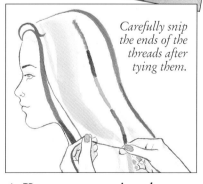

Carefully snip the ends of the threads after tying them.

4. Keep on swapping the threads all the way down to create bold stripes. Then secure the ends by tying them in a small, neat knot.

HAIR TYPES AND TREATMENTS

The sebaceous glands in your hair follicles produce oil to keep your hair healthy. If they produce too much, or too little oil, your hair may become greasy or dry.

The chart below will help you identify what type of hair you have. It will help you understand the condition of your hair and provides tips on how to look after it.

HAIR TYPE	SYMPTOMS	CAUSE	TREATMENT
Normal hair	*Normal hair is usually healthy, shiny and easy to manage. It feels soft and smooth to the touch.*	Your sebaceous glands naturally produce the correct amount of oil. This is helped by a balanced diet and plenty of exercise.	*Use a mild shampoo and a light conditioner. If your hair begins to appear damaged, give it a warm oil conditioning treatment (see page 12).*
Greasy hair	*Greasy hair looks flat and oily. It returns to this state soon after washing.*	Your sebaceous glands produce too much oil. Hair can be made greasy by running your fingers through it, too much brushing, and eating an unbalanced diet.	*Use a shampoo for greasy hair, with a high proportion of detergent to strip the scalp of grease. Apply light conditioner to ends only. Drink plenty of water.*
Dry hair	*Dry hair looks dull. It feels rough and is hard to brush. It is usually brittle, and tangles or breaks easily.*	Your sebaceous glands don't produce enough oil. Hair can also become dry as a result of bleaching, perming, heat styling or the effects of the sun.	*Use a shampoo for dry hair which has added moisturiser. Condition after every wash. Allow hair to dry naturally. Apply a warm oil treatment once a week.*
Combination hair	*If your hair is greasy at the roots and dry at the ends, it is called combination hair.*	Combination hair can be the result of colouring and bleaching, or using heated appliances which dry out the ends of the hair. Very long hair is often combination hair.	*Use a mild shampoo, concentrating on the roots of your hair. Apply conditioner to the ends only. You can buy products specially formulated for combination hair.*
Chemically-treated hair	*Hair treated with chemicals becomes dry, brittle and more difficult to manage than untreated hair.*	The chemicals used to colour and perm hair can damage the cuticle. If you use further chemicals, the damaged hair absorbs them more, causing further damage.	*Colour care shampoos and conditioners help prevent colour fading, and products for permed hair help to maintain chemical balance of the hair.*

SHAMPOOS AND CONDITIONERS

A selection of the different types of shampoos available.

TYPE	PROPERTIES	COMMENTS
pH balance	*Usually has a pH factor (see page 31) similar to that of your skin and hair, which have a pH of between 4.5 and 5.5.*	Useful for permed or coloured hair, to counteract the effects of chemicals on your hair and scalp.
Two-in-one	*Contains detergent to clean your hair and droplets of conditioner that are released to moisturise hair.*	Gives quick results because you can shampoo and condition your hair at the same time.
Herbal	*Contains extracts of various herbs and plants and is available for all hair types from dry to greasy.*	There are specific herbs you can use that benefit each type of hair.
Dry	*A shampoo in powder form which absorbs oil and dirt when brushed through dry hair.*	It takes time to remove all traces of the powder. Can leave your hair looking dull and powdery.
Anti-dandruff	*Contains chemicals that slow down the cell multiplication that causes dandruff (see page 30).*	This shampoo can dry out your hair. Use it once a week, alternating with an ordinary shampoo.
Medicated	*Contains antiseptic to kill bacteria which live on the scalp.*	Not effective on dandruff or head lice.
Insecticidal	*Contains the chemical malathion or carbaryl. These kill head lice (see page 31).*	Very harsh. Use conditioner after each treatment. You can buy special combs which remove lice eggs from your hair.

Here are some of the types of conditioner you will come across.

TYPE	PROPERTIES	COMMENTS
Rinse-out	*Creams and balsams applied after shampoo and rinsed out with water.*	Available for all types of hair, from greasy to dry.
Leave-in	*Sprays, liquids or mousses, which don't have to be rinsed out of your hair.*	Form a barrier around hair which reduces damage from heat appliances.
Hot oils	*Olive or almond oil coats the hair shaft, repairing damaged cuticles.*	Particularly good for very dry, damaged hair. To apply see page 12.
Restructurants	*Penetrate the hair and help strengthen the inner layer of the hair shaft.*	Particularly good for flat hair that is very damaged and has lost its elasticity.
Henna wax	*Thick, clear wax which leaves all types of hair shiny and manageable.*	Has an intensive moisturising effect on dry and damaged hair.

QUESTIONS AND ANSWERS

Here are some questions that are commonly asked about hair:

◆ How can I add body to my hair?

Choose shampoos and conditioners that contain substances, known as thickeners, that will coat your hair. Only use a conditioner at the ends of your hair. If you over apply conditioner, it will weigh down your hair and make it look limp and flat.

You can use a styling product to give your hair more body. Concentrate the product at the roots. If you are blow-drying your hair, lean forwards and blast your roots with warm air. This will add extra bounce. A layered hair cut will add volume to even the straightest hair.

◆ What is dandruff?

Dandruff is a condition which occurs when the skin cells of your scalp multiply too quickly. Dead cells build up and form clumps, which are stuck together with sebum. These white flakes lie close to the roots of your hair. Dandruff is often caused by stress and poor diet. Use an anti-dandruff shampoo and resist the temptation to scratch your scalp.

◆ Why does my hair break off?

Sometimes hair breaks off in clumps, leaving patches of tufty, short hair. The most common cause of this is using harsh chemicals on your hair, overusing heated appliances, brushing too vigorously, pulling your hair into tight styles, or using rubber bands. Always use fabric-covered bands, and never rub or tug at your hair.

◆ How do I stop my hair frizzing?

Frizzy hair is often dry, dull and hard to control. Hair can become frizzy if there is any moisture in the air. To avoid frizzing, use a gel when your hair is wet or a serum on dry hair to protect it. These will seal your hair and reduce the amount of moisture it absorbs from the air around you. Use a diffuser (see page 18) attached to your hair dryer to ensure that your hair dries slowly and is not blown into a frizz.

◆ Will cutting my hair make it grow faster and thicker?

No. Cutting your hair will not stimulate growth. When you have your hair cut, it may look a little thicker because any ends that have become ragged or broken are trimmed off.

◆ Can I buy a conditioner that will mend my split ends?

No. Split ends occur when a hair shaft splits in two because the hair is damaged. A conditioner will coat the hair shaft, temporarily sealing the ends. However, you can't mend ends once they are split. The only way to cure split ends is to have them cut off, so have your hair trimmed regularly.

◆ Is brushing bad for my hair?

No. Brushing distributes the natural oils along the hair shaft, conditioning your hair. However, make sure you brush your hair gently and that you use a good quality hair brush (see page 16) to avoid damaging your hair.

A GLOSSARY OF HAIR WORDS

On this page, some of the hair words you might come across are explained.

anagen - The phase of new growth in the life of a strand of hair. It lasts between two and six years.

bob – A popular, one-length hairstyle. This means that if an imaginary horizontal line was drawn around the bottom of the hair all the ends would touch it. Bobs come with or without fringes.

catagen – The period of change in the life of a hair when the sebaceous gland becomes less active and it gradually stops growing. The phase lasts about a month.

ceramide – An ingredient in many hair products which coats the cuticle of a hair, adding moisture and thickness.

dandruff – A condition in which skin cells in the scalp multiply too quickly.

head lice – Tiny lice that breed and lay eggs in hair. They cause an itchy scalp. They are caught by contact with another afflicted person. Lice breed in clean hair. Anyone can become infected, so there is no need to feel embarrassed.

highlights – A technique in which fine sections of hair are lightened with bleach to produce a natural, sun-lightened look.

keratin – The substance from which hair is built.

lighteners – Rinses or sprays which contain hydrogen peroxide. They act in the same way as bleaches (see page 23), removing colour from the cortex of the hair shaft. They are usually applied to dry or damp hair and activated by heat from a hair dryer or the sun. They can be very damaging to hair.

lowlights – A technique in which a colour that is different from the hair's natural shade is applied to small sections of the hair.

panthenol (also known as **pro-vitamin B5**) – A chemical which can make hair look thicker by adding moisture.

perming – A method of using chemicals to curl hair permanently. The hair is wrapped around rollers and a chemical solution applied to it. The chemicals break the bonds between the molecules in the hair shaft. The bonds are then reformed into the curly shape created by the rollers.

pH factor – A number used to indicate how much hydrogen a solution contains. It tells you whether the substance is alkaline or acid. The more hydrogen there is in a substance, the more alkaline it is. Skin and hair have an hydrogen content of between pH4.5 and 5.5. Products with a similar pH are best for your hair.

porous – When a hair's cuticle becomes rough or damaged, it is described as porous.

silicone – A substance that coats the hair shaft and adds extra gloss.

telogen – The phase in the life of a strand of hair during which the sebaceous gland stops working, the follicle shrinks and the hair eventually falls out. This period lasts approximately 100 days.

trichologist – A specialist who diagnoses and deals with hair and scalp problems.

CUTTING TECHNIQUES

Some of the main cutting techniques are described below.

blunt cutting – The ends of the hair are cut straight across. It is ideal for fine hair, making it look fuller and thicker. Blunt cuts are usually one length.

feathering or **slide cutting** – The stylist slides the scissors up and down small sections of hair. This makes the sections of hair thinner towards the ends.

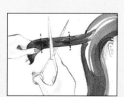

graduating – The ends of the hair are cut at an angle to the head. The hair on top looks thicker and blends with shorter hair at the back and sides.

layering – The hair is cut to different lengths. Usually the top layers are the shortest. Layering gives a rounder, softer appearance to a hairstyle.

thinning – Special thinning scissors or a razor are used to reduce the thickness or bulk of hair without changing its actual length.

INDEX

ACKNOWLEDGMENTS

Models - Hayley Biggs, Rosie Dickins, Lulu Tabbarah-Nana, Abi Taylor, Rachael Taylor, Amy Treppass, Hanna Watts, and Zoë Wray
With thanks to: Ruth King and Fiona Watt
The following companies kindly contributed equipment for the photographs in this book:- Babyliss, Belson Products, Comare, Comby, Denman, Fransen, Wahl, Charles Worthington Special thanks to Sally Hair and Beauty Supplies for hair and beauty products and Head Gardener for hair accessories

The following companies kindly contributed products for the photographs in this book:- Aveda, No 7 and 17, Jerome Russell Cosmetics Ltd, Superdrug, VO5, Wella
The following organisations kindly gave permission to reproduce their photographs:- cover – Jonathan Bokallil/Robert Harding Picture Library; page 4 – Redkin and Dr Jeremy Burgess/ Science Photo Library; page 7 – Tom Lee/Worthington salon – Covent Garden, London, UK; Wig Out – Connectix Corp., 2955 Campus Drive, San Mateo, CA 94403